SIRI®
A USER GUIDE

Published in Singapore by KINJANI

Copyright © 2016 KINJANI LLP

www.kinjani.com
contact@kinjani.com

National Library Board,
Singapore Cataloguing-in-Publication Data

Wool, Dan, author.

Siri: a user guide / Dan Wool.
Singapore, Kinjani LLP, [2016]

ISBN 978-981-09-9162-3 (paperback)

1. Siri (Electronic resource) - Handbooks, manuals, etc. 2. iPhone OS. 3. iP-
hone (Smartphone). 4. iPad (Computer). 5. iPod touch (Digital music player).

DDC 006.454 - dc23
OCN 945743159

978-981-09-9162-3

SIRI®

A USER GUIDE

Dan Wool

KINJANI

Contents

PREFACE
Your Own Personal Assistant

Growing up, I was a big fan of science fiction books. I spent hours reading and dreaming about a world where I could be in command of my own space fleet, fighting evil with my army of technologically superior robot soldiers, before returning to my city where flying cars brought people around and robots did all the hard work.

While it may take a while before these childhood visions get realised, I was excited to learn about the addition of a virtual assistant to the iPhone. While such tools had been available, it was an experiment in bringing intelligent virtual assistants to the mass market. Smartphones are indispensable tools in today's world, with the multitude of applications that help you in every area of your life.

Siri represents a way to improve and manage the way your phone fits into your schedule and workflow. While it started in a modest way with limited functions, Siri's capabilities has expanded along with the improvements in hardware and software. It is now much more powerful and sophisticated, waiting to learn to read and interpret your commands.

Properly used, Siri can be a great help. I expect virtual assistants to be increasingly integrated into our devices and hence, the way we work. This book is meant to take you through Siri's various functions, ranging from managing your contacts, quick access to your various daily applications, to sourcing for and serving up information that you need or want. The better you know your personal assistant, the more you can get out of it.

Enjoy!

Dan

INTRODUCTION
What can I help you with?

Have you ever been frustrated with trying to fumble your way through the settings and applications on your phone, or wished you could just command your phone to do as you asked? Have you been wanting your own personal assistant by your side at all times? If you have, Siri is the answer to your frustrations.

Siri is a voice-activated personal assistant found in the iPhone (4S and newer), iPad (third-generation and newer) and the iPod Touch (fifth-generation and newer).

Siri was built for talking instead of typing. It understands your voice in natural language, letting you speak to it as if you were talking to a friend or an assistant.

Siri is connected to your apps and other online services, such as Wikipedia, Shazam, Rotten Tomatoes, and Wolfram Alpha, with more likely to come. With app integration, Siri can help you take notes, set reminders or complete tasks with just your voice alone.

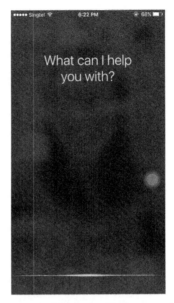

Figure 1.1   What can I help you with?

On the Apple Macintosh computers (OS X Mountain Lion and above), you also get access to Siri's functionality by using the dictation feature.

About Siri

Siri was launched on 4 October 2011 amid much fanfare, along with the iPhone 4S. It represented one of the first mainstream intelligent assistant applications that featured voice interaction with mobile devices.

Siri was the result of over 40 years of research funded by the DARPA (Defense Advanced Research Projects Agency), carried out at the Stanford Research Institute's International Artificial Intelligence Centre. Siri was first launched as an iOS app, which was then acquired by Apple in April 2010 and made into a core feature for Apple's many devices.

Siri is an improvement over traditional speech recognition technology, which featured strict vocabulary and limited accent

Figure 1.2   Siri makes it easy to place a call

recognition. Siri is able to recognise natural language, which lets you feel like you are speaking to an actual person.

The voice recognition technology adapts to your voice, tone and commands over time, letting Siri "learn" about you. Over time, Siri will get better at understanding your speech and giving you the answers you want.

Your commands are placed into context, based on user data such as your location, open applications or relationships. This lets Siri tailor its responses to what it thinks you need. Its ability to recognise context has been further enhanced with iOS 9 and Proactive, letting it predict what you need based on your usage history.

The latest updates to Siri include expanded language settings. It is now able to speak in non-English languages such as Mandarin, Spanish and Italian, although functionality may be limited. The full list of languages can be accessed on Apple's website or on your device.

Some features in iOS 9 are not available in every country; for example, restaurant reservations are only available in Canada, Mexico and USA.

iOS 9

With iOS 9, Siri has received a promotion! Spotlight has now been subsumed by Siri, which has gotten a nice little upgrade. Apple claims that Siri has gotten about 40% more accurate since iOS 8, along with improvements in both speed and error rates. Industry surveys have pitched Siri against competitors Google Now and Microsoft's Cortana, and awarded Siri top spot for its accuracy and comprehension.

With the new Siri, the search feature is now consistent across text and voice. Regardless of which you choose, you will be able to search using natural language, typing or speaking as though you were conversing with a person. The Spotlight search page on your devices has been replaced with a Siri search screen, incorporating Proactive and allowing Siri to understand and predict what you need.

Figure 1.3   Get quick app suggestions

Proactive means that Siri will now feed you with suggested items: apps, nearby places, news, and contacts. Some examples of Proactive in action include:

- Suggestions for recipients when you create a new email
- Automatically add an event to your Calendar
- Quick links to apps that you use at a certain time or place
- Plug in to CarPlay and get your usual podcast loaded up
- Get a playlist loaded up when you plug in your earphones
- Possible identities for unidentified callers

Figure 1.4   Your music loads when you
insert your earphones

Version History

Siri has seen many changes since its initial launch, with new features added at every iOS upgrade. Apple is working to make Siri a key way to interact with the Apple Watch, so expect even more features on that front. Here is a list of some changes in each version.

iOS 6
- Make reservations through OpenTable
- Search for sports statistics, movie reviews
- Update Facebook status or send tweets
- Launch applications
- Dictate text and emails

iOS 7
- New layered look that fades into current view
- More human-like speech, with male and female voices
- Access Settings, Wikipedia, Bing, Twitter
- Upgraded Twitter integration
- Name learning, display missed calls, read out emails

iOS 8
- Can be used with Apple Music ("Play the top songs from 1982", "Play more songs like this", "After this song, play 'Coldplay'")
- Activate Siri with "Hey Siri"
- Real time visual feedback when speaking

- Song ID feature

iOS 9
- New interface that looks like Siri on Apple Watch
- Improved contextual awareness, tied to Proactive (using your location, time of day, recurring activity, apps currently open, connected devices, etc. for context)
- Using Proactive, Siri will try to provide assistance before you ask
- Search photos and videos (using dates, locations, album titles)
- Spotlight has largely been subsumed by Siri
- Reminders – If you see something, you can say "Remind me about this" and Siri will set a reminder linked to the original content

watchOS 2
- Check your Glances
- Start a specific workout
- Look up words in the dictionary

Figure 1.5   Go ahead...

Privacy Issues

Siri works by processing your commands on its servers, storing user data improve accuracy and recognition. This allows Siri to learn over time – the longer you use it, the better it works.

Siri uses user data that is tied to a randomised identifier on your device instead of your Apple ID. This includes contacts, songs in your library, and your location when you make the request (if you have Location Services turned on). The Apple Watch uses the identifier from your associated iPhone. Because of this unique, random identifier, Siri cannot be consistent across devices.

Each device has unique data associated only with that device. When you turn Siri off, the user data associated with that device is deleted. This means that when you restart Siri, it will have to restart the learning process. This makes Siri a little different from similar intelligent personal assistants offered by Google (Google Now) and Microsoft (Cortana).

Both Google Now and Cortana are cloud-based services, storing your profile and preferences on the cloud and allowing them to be applied across your devices. The only exception is data available on local apps that have access to the cloud. For example, Siri is able to access the Calendar app on your iPhone, which could contain data consistent across all your devices.

According to Apple, your voice recordings are kept for up to 2 years. Once it is 6 months old, Apple dissociates your identifier from the voice clip, and keeps it for up to 18 months for testing and product improvement.

Apple's stance on privacy partly restricts Siri's ability to fully understand its user. For example, both Google Now and Cortana tap into your search and browsing history on Google and Bing respectively, but Siri doesn't use data from these sources at all.

The use of location history is also different across these services. While location history logging is mandatory for Cortana and an opt-out service on Google, Siri only uses the history available on your device. An iPad that only sits on the kitchen table at home will learn a lot less about you than the iPhone you carry around.

SETUP & FEATURES
I'm Siri, your virtual assistant.

Siri is already part of the iPhone and iPad operating system, so you don't need to download anything. To access the Siri menu, navigate to Settings -> General -> Siri. Once activated, you will see a menu with several options.

Figure 2.1   Accessing Siri's settings

Options

Language: Select your preferred language. When it was first launched, the only options available were English (Australia, U.S., U.K.), French, and German. The list of supported has expanded to include more languages and local accents.

In iOS 9.2, Siri supports:

- Arabic
- English (Australia, Canada, India, New Zealand, Singapore, U.K., U.S.)
- Chinese (Cantonese, Mandarin–China, Mandarin–Taiwan)
- Danish
- Dutch (Belgium, Netherlands)
- French (Belgium, Canada, France, Switzerland)
- German (Austria, Germany, Switzerland)
- Italian (Italy, Switzerland)
- Japanese
- Korean
- Norweigian Bokmål
- Portuguese (Brazil)
- Russian
- Spanish (Mexico, Spain, U.S.)
- Swedish
- Thai
- Turkish.

Support for Arabic comes with an update to the latest iOS (as of this writing), iOS 9.2.

Figure 2.2   Language options

Voice Gender: Choose a male or female voice. This setting is only available for certain languages (English, German and Japanese).

Accent: This setting is only available for certain languages. For English, American, Australian and British accents are available.

Voice Feedback: Select whether you want to hear Siri's responses (Always On), only when your ringer is switched on (Control with Ring Switch), or only when using a hands-free option (Hands-free Only). If you only want Siri to respond with text, select Hands-free Only. The Control with Ring Switch option is new to iOS 9. With this setting, you will not hear Siri's response if your iPhone or iPad is set to silent.

My Info: Here you can select your own contact information by pointing to yourself in your Contacts. Siri will call you by your name (although you can tell it to call you something else). Your information is used by Siri in several ways, including setting up relationships and to provide directions.

Raise to Speak: This option is only available on iPhones running iOS 7 and before. If enabled, lets you talk to Siri by raising your iPhone to your ear. In later versions, this has been replaced by "Hey Siri". This allows you to activate Siri by saying "Hey, Siri", although your device has to be connected to a power supply for iPhone 6 and earlier.

Calling for Siri

In order to use Siri effectively, you will need two things:

1. *An Internet connection.* Siri records your voice and transfers it to Apple servers, where it is interpreted and returned to your phone. This requires an Internet connection even for a local task, such as noting down a reminder or changing your settings.

2. *Decent recording quality.* Siri needs to be able to pick up your words to accurately determine your instructions. Speak clearly, slowly and with as little background noise as possible to improve your success rate.

Because of the way Siri works by sending your recording over the Internet, it will require cellular data or a WiFi connection to process. If Siri cannot access the Internet, it will inform you by saying "Sorry, I am having trouble connecting to the Internet" or a variation of this message. Should this happen, check on your Internet connection and try again.

You can launch Siri in several ways:
1. Press and hold the Home button
2. Say "Hey Siri"
3. Press the control button from your headset, or car kit
4. Raise to Speak (only available for iPhones running iOS 7 and earlier).

Say "Hey Siri"
one more time

Set Up "Hey Siri" Later

Figure 2.3   Siri training

With iPhone 6/iOS 8.4 and earlier, the "Hey Siri" command
only works when the device is plugged into a power source, as
it will have to constantly scan for your command. If you own
an iPhone 6S or 6S Plus, the "Hey Siri" function will work even
without being plugged in. You can also engage in Siri training,
letting Siri detect and get used to your speech.

Once you activate Siri, you will hear a high-pitched chime,
which indicates that Siri is listening. The bottom button will
transform into a wave, which swings higher when your voice is

received. Siri detects the pauses in your input in order to guess the end of your instruction.

Once it is done listening, Siri will play a higher-pitched chime to acknowledge your input. If no input is provided, Siri will play a low-pitched chime to indicate that it has stopped listening.

Figure 2.4   Bye-bye Siri!

Bye-bye Siri: You can exit Siri by saying "Bye-bye" or pressing the home button. Several other commands will work too.

- Dismiss Siri

- Close Siri
- Goodbye
- So long
- Bye

Saying "Cancel" will exit whatever Siri is doing, while "Restart" begins a new dialogue with Siri. This is useful when you want to move on to a different command. You can also cancel your request by tapping the microphone icon.

Speaking to Siri: Siri has been programmed to cater to natural language, allowing you to speak naturally without a fixed set of vocabulary. That said, there are ways to improve your success rate with Siri's voice-recognition technology.

1. Environment

Make sure that Siri can hear you clearly. It might be difficult to decipher your input if you are in a noisy or windy area. If Siri does not receive your input, try bringing your device closer to you or increasing your volume. If this happens repeatedly, check that the microphone is not blocked by your finger or your phone case.

2. Clarity

Siri works best when it can easily decipher the spaces between your words, so try to enunciate as clearly as possible. If you are having difficulty being understood, try slowing down your sentence, emphasising your words and adding short pauses between each word.

3. Be Specific
Be as specific as you can with your instructions. While Siri will adjust for contextual information, it helps to be specific to ensure you get the right response. For example, when setting an alarm, include the AM/PM so that Siri will recognise the right time to set your alarm.

4. Structure
Siri is built for natural language processing, so you don't have to tweak your sentence structures to suit Siri's vocabulary, unless your colloquial-speak is quite incomprehensible! Siri is also capable of recognising and recording inflection and tones. Speaking naturally with such tones will help improve your recognition rate.

While Siri can perform some self-correction when you finish your sentence, it is best to rely on clear speech to avoid having to correct it later. Note that Siri looks out for pauses to determine the end of your input, so don't pause too long!

Corrections: Siri lets you correct your input if it misinterpreted you. After you finish speaking, your input will appear on your screen. Tap the line to begin editing it. Once you have finished, press "Done" to send your new instructions. You can also edit it using your voice by tapping on the microphone symbol on the keyboard.

Figure 2.5   Corrections

Besides correcting your inputs this way, you can correct your text messages or emails using voice instructions. For example, to rewrite your message, say "Change it to: Tomorrow is Thursday." You can also redirect your item by saying "No, send to David" when Siri asks for a confirmation.

Note, however, that you can't edit things that have already been written into your apps. For example, after creating a note ("Note that tomorrow is Wednesday"), trying to edit it to "Tomorrow is Thursday" will return an error message. You can, however, add on more material to your existing item.

Figure 2.6   Rewriting your message

Your Results: When you get Siri to perform an action, a new item will appear on your screen where applicable. These items allow interaction if they involve other applications. For example, when you get Siri to set an alarm for 7AM ("Wake me up at 7AM"), it will show you the alarm with the on/off toggle. If you ask Siri to create a note ("Note that tomorrow is Wednesday"), the note will appear on your screen. Tapping it will send you to the Notes application.

Some items do not allow for interaction, however, such as when you ask for the definition of "pluralistic" ("What is the meaning

Figure 2.7   Quick access to your settings

of pluralistic"). A dictionary definition will appear, but tapping on this will not direct you to any applications.

This feature can be very useful. With this, you can navigate your phone quickly without having to access individual menus. For example, to access the Siri menu in Settings, simply say "Show me the settings for Siri."

Hey Siri, call me Your Majesty

You can get Siri to call you something else other than your name. To do this, launch Siri and say "Call me Your Majesty." Siri will reply with a confirmation, and address you by your chosen nickname. Don't be shy, you know you want to experiment, so go ahead!

Figure 2.8   Your Majesty, how can I help?

If Siri gets your name wrong, don't fret, you can always correct it. Just say "That's not how you pronounce my name." When you do that, Siri will run through each word in your name, ask you for your pronunciation, then verify that it got the pronunciation correct. While this does help improve name recognition, it isn't perfect, especially if your name is uncommon or has different tones.

Figure 2.9   That's not how you pronounce my name..

Over time, Siri will learn to recognise the patterns in your accent and speech. It also uses contextual clues in your phone, such as your apps and contacts, in order to decipher your instructions.

As you continue using Siri, it will understand you better and improve your recognition rate. However, your user data will be deleted once you disable Siri in your Settings. You will have to rebuild this your profile again if you choose to restart it.

KEEPING IN TOUCH
Siri, I am your father..

The phone helps you in touch with all your contacts, and Siri lets you do that with ease. Using Siri, you have access to all your contacts, allowing you to send text messages, emails and update your social media profiles using your voice.

You can set up your relationships with other people too. With knowledge of your network, Siri can help you contact the people you want to talk to using these relationships.

Setting up your Relationships

Setting up your network lets you personalise your interactions with Siri and use it as a shortcut. For example, once you tell Siri which contact refers to your mother, you can call her by saying "Call Mother." It's as easy as that.

There are two ways to set up your relationships:

1. Using Siri
    Tell Siri about your relationships with others by indicating the contact and the relationship. "John Roberts is my father" will

identify the contact John Roberts as your father. This information is captured and stored in your list of contacts in the
Contacts app.

Figure 3.1   List of relationships

The default settings provide a list of relationships to choose
from (mother, father, parent, brother, sister, child, friend,
spouse, partner, assistant, manager, other), but you can go
beyond this list, as long as the relationship can be recognised.
"Peter Gabriels is my doctor" will set up that relationship.
Even something quirky like "Sandy Williams is my teacup"

will work too. The only requirement is that the person you are adding must already be in your list of contacts.

If Siri makes a mistake or cannot understand you, you can edit the relationship label through your Contacts.

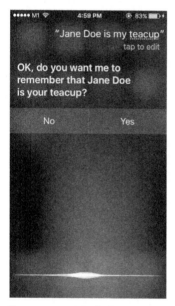

Figure 3.2   My darling teacup

2.   From Contacts

You can also set up relationships using contact information in Contacts. To do so, go to your contact information and tap "Edit" on the top right. Scroll down to an option called "add related name." Here you can add your relationships by selecting individual contacts and specifying the relationship. If you want a customised label, scroll to the bottom of the list, where there is an option to "Add Custom Label."

Once you have your relationships set up, you can start using them within Siri. "Call my doctor" or "Dial my doctor" will initiate a call to your doctor. This works with other types of instructions, such "Send a message to my lover."

Warning: Any relationships that you add to your Contact will be included if you send someone else your Contact card. If you intend to share your Contact card but wish to keep your information private, remember to create a second Contact without that information.

Who should I ring for you?

Calling with Siri is easy and intuitive. You can either name your recipient and his/her specific number (mobile, home, etc.), use a relationship label, or read out a phone number. If you are trying to place an international call, add the country code in front by saying "Plus One," if the code is +1. Siri can also help you make a Facetime call.

Figure 3.3   Facetime calls with Siri

It helps to be as specific as you can. If you have several contacts that share the same first name (James Wilson, James Blake, James

Blank), include the last name when you instruct Siri. If not, Siri will clarify first before dialing.

- Call James
- Call James Blank
- Call my mother
- Dial home
- Dial Tom on his mobile
- Dial Lindsey on her work phone
- Call 212-555-2368
- Call +62 6999 9100 (say plus-six-two-six...)
- Facetime Jenny

Who would you like to text?

Siri can help you check your text messages, reply to them and compose new ones. You can even get your unread messages read out to you! With Siri's help, you can connect with your contacts on the go, hands-free.

All types of messages are supported, including messages sent using iMessage. There are several ways to start composing your message. Siri recognises certain key words such as Tell, Message, or Text.

You can compose a message the long way, by instructing Siri to "Message my father." Siri replies with a cue to dictate your text message. Once you're done, it shows you the message and asks for a confirmation before sending it. You can choose to cancel your message with "Cancel", get Siri to re-read your message with "Review" or "Read it again", or amend your message or recipient.

- No, send it to my mother
- Add I'll be back full stop (this adds "I'll be back." to your message)
- Change to I'll be there soon

Once you are satisfied, say "Send" or "Continue". Siri will follow up by saying "Sent" or something similar. If you reply "No" to Siri's request for confirmation, your message will be kept on the screen. From here, you can either "Continue" or "Send" it, "Cancel" or "Review" to re-read your message again.

Figure 3.4   Confirming your message

Siri is capable of composing the entire message with just one line of instruction, as long as you include a recipient and some content. Siri also allows you to send multiple recipients at the same time. Remember, be as specific as possible. If your recipient has more than one number stored, specify which number (home, mobile, etc.) to send your message to.

- Tell Susan I'll be late
- Tell James on his mobile that I'll be late

- Message my wife hello
- Message hello to my wife
- Send a message to Peter hello
- Send a message to 212-555-2368 that I'm almost there
- Tell Jenny and Jack I'll be there in 20 minutes

Reading messages

Figure 3.5   Read me my messages

Siri can read the messages that you receive on your devices, and let you respond to them with your voice. With this feature, you can reply or keep track of your text messages hands-free. If you have "Hey Siri" enabled, you won't even have to tap anything to access your new messages.

Once you activate Siri (using "Hey Siri" or by holding down the home key), tell Siri, "Read me my messages" or "Read message".

Siri will then read out all unread text messages in order. If you need to hear it again, just tell Siri to "Read it again".

When Siri is done reading, it will prompt you for a reply. You will have to include an action word ("Reply", "Text" or "Tell") to send it. Otherwise, Siri will treat your response as separate input. Siri will then ask for your confirmation before sending out your reply.

Figure 3.6   Just two mins late

Alternatively, you can also tell Siri to "Call him". Siri will then access your contacts and dial the sender. Note that variations such as "Call" or "Call sender" will not work. Instead, Siri will attempt to search your contacts for one named "sender".

- Reply I'll be two minutes late
- Tell her I'm on my way
- Call him

Writing Emails

There are a few ways to compose your emails. To do it the long way, tell Siri to "Send an email" or just "Email". Siri will ask for a recipient, then a subject, followed by the message. Once this is done, Siri will ask for your confirmation before sending it out.

Figure 3.7   Email screen

You can speed things up by including more details. Siri is able to take long instructions, as long as the recipient, subject and content are clearly separated. One way to include all your details is to tell Siri to "Email [recipient] about the [subject] and say [content]". This produces a complete email that can be sent once confirmed.

Any variation of this instruction will work. As with text-based messages, you can use relationship information or nicknames in your commands. Be as specific as possible, specifying which email address to send to if there are multiple addresses.

You can also include CC and BCC fields in your instructions. Say "Email [recipient]", then a pause, "CC [CC recipient]", then your content. Your recipients should be available in your device's Contacts. You can also say "carbon copy" or "blind carbon copy" instead. I find that this works better than using "CC".

If your recipient is not in your Contacts, you can direct Siri to email them by saying the entire email address. While this does work, it is quite tricky to pull off, as Siri will try to look in your address book for someone it recognises based on what you say.

Here are some examples:

- Email Jackson about the missing dog
- Mail my father about tonight's plans
- Email Jason home about the change in structure (This sends an email to Jason's home email address)
- Email dad and mom about the new house and say, come over tonight, exclamation point (This produces an email with the message "Come over tonight!")

- Email Mike carbon copy Lindy subject tomorrow's plans

Siri is able to understand punctuation, although you should add in short pauses to ensure that it interprets your instructions. More about punctuation and other useful commands can be found at the end of this chapter and in the reference at the back of the book.

Figure 3.8   Cc and Bcc

Checking your Emails

Siri can also help you check your email. This function has been improved since iOS 7. Previously, Siri could only send your emails. With the upgraded iOS, Siri can now read out your list of emails, read the contents of your emails, and allow you to reply to them.

To check your latest emails, simply tell Siri to "Show me my emails" or "Check my emails". Siri will return a list of your latest emails.

Figure 3.9   Show me my emails

When you tell Siri to show you emails, it will return with a list. You can instruct Siri to read out the subject and/or contents of your emails. When you say "Read my emails", Siri will read out the sender, time received and subject of the first three emails, followed by a question "Would you like to hear the entire list?"

You can also select specific emails to be read out to you. Do this by saying "Read the first email" or "Read the latest email". After reading out an email, Siri will ask "Do you want to reply?" Say yes to bring up the reply function. To forward the email instead, say "Forward e-mail to Jackson". Siri will then prompt you for an additional message that you can include.

Social media integration

Siri is now on social media! Since iOS 6, Siri has been integrated with Facebook and Twitter, allowing you to post updates directly using Siri.

Note: Using Siri to post directly will only work if you have set up your Facebook or Twitter accounts in Settings. If you haven't already done so, go to the settings menu and scroll down to the social media section. The settings for both applications can be found there.

Figure 3.10   Write on my wall

Figure 3.11   Tweet!

To post a status update, say something like "Post to Facebook", "Update my Facebook status" or "Write on my wall". Siri will then prompt you for your message. You can also say both the instructions and your message in one breath. Once you're done, Siri will confirm your message before posting it.

Twitter works the same way. Using Siri, you can insert location and hashtags too. To start sending a tweet, say "Tweet" or "Post to Twitter" followed by your message. Siri will let you preview your message and ask for a confirmation before sending it.

To include your location, shout the command "Tweet with my location". Siri's preview of the tweet will include a small arrow with your location tag. Note that for this to work, you will have to allow Twitter to access your location.

If you want to add a hashtag, simply say "hashtag" followed by your keyword. This will work regardless of where you place your hashtag, in mid-sentence or at the end.

Siri can also check your tweets for you. To do so, say "Show me my tweets". This will bring up a list of your tweets from your Twitter account. To search for subject-related tweets, include the subject in your instructions. "Show me tweets about Obama" will return a list of tweets that match the keyword "Obama".

While this works for Twitter, Siri cannot search Facebook or check your Facebook timeline for you. You can, however, launch the Facebook app from Siri by saying "Open Facebook".

Finding friends

If you (and your friends) have Find My Friends enabled, Siri can access that feature to give you a list of locations or people. You can use broad commands like "Where are my friends" or specific commands, such as "Is my husband at home?"

Figure 3.12   My husband better be at home

If you ask Siri something like "Where are my friends?" it will produce a list of people around you and their distance from you. Asking specific questions such as "Find me my brother" or "Where's my wife" will return specific locations.

Figure 3.13　Where are my friends?

This is only possible if you and your contacts have Find My Friends activated, and are actively sharing your locations. That said, having the feature turned on all the time will drain your battery much quicker.

Period, exclamation point!

You can include punctuation in your instructions to Siri, even smiley faces! Siri can also take formatting commands and basic mathematical or currency symbols. These are especially useful if you use Dictation frequently.

Here are some commands you can use. A longer list can be found at the back of the book.

Formatting Commands

New line	Inserts a line break and starts on a new line (equivalent to pressing Enter on a keyboard)
New paragraph	Starts on a new paragraph
Caps on	Capitalises the first letter of each word until turned off
Caps off	Turn off "Caps on"
No space on	Stop adding spaces to your instructions. This helps with spelling your word if it's not easily recognised
No space off	Revert to normal spaces between words
Quote... end quote	Places quotation marks around a section of text
Open single quote... close single quote	Places single quotation marks around a section of text

Punctuation

Period / dot	.
Comma	,
Exclamation mark / point	!
Inverted exclamation mark / point	¡
Question mark	?
Ellipsis / dot dot dot	...
Hyphen / dash	-
Em dash	–
Underscore	_
Open parenthesis	(
Close parenthesis	)
Open bracket	[
Close bracket	]
Ampersand	&
Slash / forward slash	/
Backward slash	\
Quote / quotation mark	"
Single quote	'

Mathematical Functions / Currency

Plus sign	+
Minus sign	-
Equals sign	=
Greater than sign	>
Lesser than sign	<
Percent sign	%
Euro sign	€
Yen sign	¥
Dollar sign	$
Pound sterling sign	£
Cent sign	¢

Figure 3.14   Smiley faces

Siri can also produce smileys with "smiley face", "frowny face", "wink face" or "cross-eyed laughing face". The selection is quite limited, but you can always read out punctuation symbols to get the expression you want! Besides the selection of smileys, Siri also recognises certain abbreviations. For example, reading out the letters "e g" or "i e" will also produce "e.g." and "i.e."

YOUR PERSONAL ASSISTANT
At your service, master

The smartphone and its applications have taken the place many of their physical counterparts. Your phone can now serve as your organiser, helping you take notes, send reminders, wake you up in the morning and help you keep track of your calendar.

With Siri, you can access your applications on the go, without having to tap to enter each application separately. Setting your alarm or noting down an idea is now a breeze.

Your contacts

The smartphone is now a portable phone book, storing your lists of contacts and their individual information. Accessing your Contacts using Siri is quick and simple. You can access specific information within each Contact card.

- Show me John Wilkinson
- What is John's home number
- What is Johnson's mobile
- What is Wendy's email address

- When is Lindy's birthday
- What is my father's address

Figure 4.1 Show me Bossman

Keeping time

Siri can help you access Clock, Alarm and Timer functions very quickly. Unfortunately, Siri cannot access the Stopwatch. Asking it to "Start a five-minute stopwatch" will only provide you with a link to launch your Stopwatch.

Figure 4.2 Be my alarm clock

To set an alarm for 7AM, say "Wake me up at 7AM tomorrow". Your alarm and the on/off toggle will be shown on your screen, letting you turn it off if you wish to cancel it. Being specific with AM or PM will help Siri interpret your instructions better.

Siri can also set your alarm based on hour or minute commands, or delete your alarms for you. Cancelling your alarm switches it off, while deleting it will remove the notification completely.

- Wake me up at 7AM tomorrow
- Wake me up in two hours
- Set an alarm for thirty minutes
- Show me my alarms
- Change my 4PM alarm to 430PM
- Cancel my 8AM alarm

Setting a timer

Siri can be used to set a timer quickly. Tell Siri to "Set a timer" followed by the duration when prompted, or say "Set a timer for 20 minutes". The timer will be shown on your screen and start counting down immediately. Tap the timer to open the Timer application.

Figure 4.3   Setting a timer

You can show, adjust or stop the timer easily with Siri. Try the following commands:

- Show the timer
- Change timer to 20 minutes (This starts a new 20-minute timer)
- Pause timer
- Cancel timer
- Resume timer

Checking the time

Getting Siri to check the time for you might not sound useful, but it could come in handy when you need it hands-free. You can ask for both date and time by saying "What is the date", "What year is it" or "What time is it?"

Siri's time functions can be useful when you need to check the time in another timezone. It can also help you count the number of days to a certain date, or the date on another day.

Figure 4.4   Time in Chicago

Figure 4.5   Can't wait till Christmas!

- What is the time
- What time is it in New York
- What time is it in New Delhi
- What is the time in Singapore 8 hours from now
- What is today's date
- What is the date this Friday
- How many days until Labour Day
- How many days until fifth December

Show me my appointments

Figure 4.6   Setting up an appointment

Calendars in iOS and OS X can be synced using iCloud, making organising your events and appointments a lot easier. Siri lets you access Calendar functions using voice commands, giving you greater convenience in managing your schedule.

To add a new Calendar entry, use a keyword such as "Set up" or "Schedule", followed by details about the appointment. You can specify details such as location, time, the subject of your meeting and who you are meeting with. Siri can also take instructions about the duration of the event. If no directions are given, the default duration is set at 1 hour.

Depending on your plans, you can be as concise as "Meet 8PM" to add a generic event for the evening. Here are some examples:

- Meet with Robert at 8PM tomorrow
- Appointment with Susan tomorrow at 3PM about the new house
- Schedule a meeting with Lisa at noon tomorrow
- Set up a discussion with the board for 12PM next Friday
- Arrange a meeting at 8PM on 3rd October 2015
- Set up a meeting about the new plans from 9AM to 11AM tomorrow

If your appointment clashes with an existing event, Siri will ask to confirm the details again before adding it to your calendar.

Siri can help change or cancel your scheduled appointments. This can be done much quicker than using the Calendar app itself! You can also add or remove people from your meeting, or change the location of your event. Try some of the following phrases:

- Move my 2PM meeting to 4PM
- Reschedule my 3PM event for 330PM
- Cancel my 1PM appointment
- Delete my 1 o'clock tomorrow

- Add James to the 6PM meeting on Friday
- Change location of 8PM meeting today to Royal Gardens
- Change location of 7PM dinner tonight to father's house
- You can take a quick look at your calendar using Siri. One of the most useful functions of Siri is being able to search your calendar for specific appointments. With Siri, you no longer have to scroll through all your appointments to find that 15-minute discussion with Steve on Friday next month. Just ask Siri, "Show me my meetings with Steve" to find it.

Figure 4.7   Move your appointments easily

Figure 4.8   View your schedule

Siri also helps you check your daily calendar and lets you query the time and location of specific events.

- Show me my calendar for tomorrow
- What do I have for this Friday
- When is my next meeting
- Where is my meeting with Mandy
- Where am I meeting Jason this Friday

Tell me what you want to be reminded about

Reminders are a great way to keep track of your to-do list. It might take some getting used to, but after you get the hang of it, it will become an indispensable aid.

Siri makes Reminders even easier to use. Reminders can make use of your location to tailor reminders to a specific place. For example, you can set a reminder to buy a new toothbrush the next time you're at the grocery store, or be reminded to print out a report when you reach the office the next day.

While location services does work with Reminders, it might need some tweaking to ensure that it works accurately with the stores in your area. You will have to update your addresses in Contacts, and allow location services to be available at all times.

Setting a reminder with Siri is easy, and Siri will prompt you for a time if you don't include it in your instructions. You can use several variations of the same command, as long as you include the keyword "Remind" or "Remember".

You can also set recurring reminders with Siri by including a phrase like "every Wednesday". Like other commands, Siri will preview your reminder and prompt for a confirmation before proceeding.

- Remind me to call my mother (This will prompt Siri to ask you for a time

- Remind me to go to the gym at 5PM tomorrow
- In 2 hours remind me to read the housing report
- Remember to buy a present for Jane at 4PM today
- Remind me to ask Jack about his trip when I reach the office
- Remind me to call Switzerland when I get home
- Remind me to buy the morning newspaper every Saturday
- Remind me to call Jensen when I'm at the car
- Remember to park at lot number 616 when I reach Frank's house

Figure 4.9   Reminders are easy to set

Reminders are synced across iCloud, so your reminders are available across all your devices. You can get Siri to show you your reminders by saying "Show me my reminders today" or asking "Do I have any reminders today?"

Your reminders for the day can be easily accessed by pulling out the notifications tab on your device. Siri comes in handy when you want to filter your notifications by date, subject or location. You can do so by asking "Show me my reminders for next week", "Do I have any reminders about the dentist" or "Do I have any reminders at the office?"

Remind me about This

With iOS 9, you are now able to set reminders about what you are currently working on. If you're in your Messages app and reading a message, you can now tell Siri to "remind me about this" or "remind me about this when I get to the car." Siri will set a reminder that includes a link back to the original message. There are several apps that currently support this, including Messages, Notes, Safari, Mail, with the list set to grow over time. This feature works with all the location features available with Reminders.

What would you like your note to say?

Just like Reminders, Siri can also work with the Notes app on your devices. Your notes are also synced across iCloud, so you can have Siri take a note on your phone while driving, and check it on your MacBook later. Siri makes note-taking much easier, letting you do it on the go with just a tap.

Create a note with Siri is easy, such as "Note that the refrigerator repairman is coming next Wednesday", "Note, replace batteries in flashlight" or "Make a note about the Heebie-Jeebies concert next month". This instruction creates a new note containing your message.

Once you have given Siri your message, it will show a preview of your note. You can add additional items to it by saying "Add", followed by your message. You can also do this with existing notes, if you know the name of the note. For example, add a new item to your To-Do list by saying "Add buy new batteries to my To-Do List note".

Unfortunately, Siri only allows you to add something to your note. If you try to get Siri to delete or edit your note, it will tell you that it cannot do so. You can only delete or edit messages through the Notes application.

Siri can help you search for your existing notes, or show you a list of all your notes. Tell Siri to "Show me all my notes" to display all your notes, or specify which notes to filter by saying "Show me shopping notes", which will bring up notes with the word 'shopping' in them.

Figure 4.10   Adding to your To-Do list

Your notes will be displayed in chronological order from newest to oldest. You can also search for notes for a given date by stating it, "Show me notes from June 16" or "Show me notes from today".

Siri can now read your notes out for you. When you instruct it to "Show me my notes", it will read the contents of the first note and ask if you want the next note read out. Tapping any of your notes will open it up in the Notes application.

Searching for photos

With iOS 9, Siri now allows you to search for photos using dates, album names or keywords. This feature uses the native search function within Photos. For example, you can bring up your photos from November by saying "Show me my pictures from November". As with many of Siri's functions, you will have to unlock your phone before you can access your photos.

Figure 4.11   Only works if you went there..

- Show me my pictures from 14 October
- Show me pictures from my Favourites

- Search for pictures taken from my location
- Show me pictures from my holiday in Quebec last October
- Show me photos I took yesterday
- Look up my videos from Boulder
- Show me the photos I took at Cape Town

Launching applications

If you have lots of apps installed on your phone and find it a bother to scroll through your multiple screens, Siri will be your lifesaver. Using Siri, you can launch any applications with the keyword "Launch" or "Open". Just say "Launch Mail" to open up your mailbox. The usual security features still apply, so you will still have to type your passcode or use Touch ID if your phone hasn't been unlocked.

Figure 4.12   Some apps require your phone
to be unlocked

AT YOUR FINGERTIPS
Your everyday tools in one place

The introduction of the smartphone has made previously tedious tasks a whole lot easier. There is a growing range of applications on all your mobile devices to help you navigate your daily routine with ease. Siri takes all that one step further, giving you a way to access these functions with just your voice.

When you're out with Siri, you can get information on the go, whether it's checking the weather before you leave, doing some quick sums before a meeting, or doing a quick search on the fly.

Siri is integrated with several online services to help you search better. This section includes an introduction to search functions, which give you access to integrated platforms such as Yelp and Wolfram Alpha. But first, let's check out the weather.

It doesn't look so nice today

Siri doesn't like the rain! Getting the weather forecast with Siri is simple and quick. You can get the weather for different dates and locations, and even a breakdown by time for today's weather.

There are many ways to ask Siri about the weather. You can also

Figure 5.1   What is today's weather?

ask for specific details, such as temperature, wind speed, wind chill, and even sunrise and sunset times. However certain details are not available for date ranges that are too far out. Siri can only check the weather 10 days ahead.

Siri uses your current location to get answers to questions that don't specify a location. It also retains the location for questions that come after each other, so remember to specify your current location (keywords "here" or "local") after asking a question about a different place. For example, if you ask "What is the humidity" after asking "What is the temperature in Denver now", it will return the humidity index for Denver.

Figure 5.2   More than just temperature

- What is today's weather (This will show an hourly forecast for the day)
- What's the forecast for tomorrow
- Show me the weather for the week
- Check the forecast for Cupertino, California this week
- Will it rain in Washington, D.C. this week

- Will I need a jacket tonight (This shows the low of the day)
- Will it snow in Boston this week
- What is the high in Milan tomorrow
- How windy is it now
- What is the windspeed here
- What time will the sun rise tomorrow in Beijing
- What is the windchill in Christchurch
- What is the humidity in Liverpool
- What is the barometric air pressure now
- What is the UV index now

Unfortunately, Siri can't get you any weather information for Antarctica. But it says sorry!

Figure 5.3   Will I need a jacket?

Searching with Siri

Searching using Siri just takes some asking. When you pose a question to Siri, it will check to see if they fit any of the integrated services, such as Wolfram Alpha, Yelp, Shazam or Wikipedia. If your query cannot be answered by these services, Siri will submit it to the search engine Bing. You can also get Siri perform a web search immediately by using the phrase "Search for" before your query.

Figure 5.4   I want kittens

With the integrated sites, your results are shown directly in the

the Siri interface. If Siri performs a web search using your search terms, it will display a list of top results. Clicking any of them will open those sites in the browser. If you scroll down to the bottom of the results, Siri will also offer to search using other sources, including on Twitter.

You can also search for pictures using Siri by using "Search for pictures of kittens" or "Show me pictures of kittens". When you ask Siri to show you the latest news about a topic, it will look for items matching those terms on Twitter.

Apple has now integrated a dictionary function with Siri. For example, you can ask Siri for the definition of "autodidact" with the query "What does autodidact mean" or "Define autodidact".

Wolfram?

Siri is integrated with Wolfram Alpha, an application that calls itself a "computational knowledge engine". With Wolfram Alpha, Siri gives you access to a giant store of data that can answer a whole range of questions. Your questions are answered directly in the Siri interface, so you don't have to open your browser or another application to use this feature.

The Wolfram Alpha database is extensive, with a wide range of topics such as Chemistry, Sports, Geography and Mathematics. When you field a question that can be answered by Wolfram, Siri will automatically submit a query and return your answer.

Alternatively, you can include a keyword before your question, such as "Wolfram" or "Ask Wolfram" instead. With this, your query will be sent directly to Wolfram Alpha without Siri trying to interpret your question beforehand.

Here are some things you can ask Siri using Wolfram Alpha:

- How far is Venus from Earth
- When was the previous solar eclipse
- How far away is the moon
- Show me the constellation of the Cassiopeia
- What is the fifth highest mountain in the world
- What is the height of Mount Kilimanjaro
- How deep is the Atlantic Ocean

Figure 5.5   Morse for chicken pie

- What is the largest ocean in the world
- What is the population of Mexico
- Square root 68
- Graph y = 8x + 8
- What is the melting point of copper
- How many calories are there in a McChicken burger
- How many calories in a small apple
- What is the price of diesel
- Show me flights overhead in Chicago

- How many days until Christmas
- How many days to 6 February 2081
- What is Morse code for chicken pie
- What is the scientific name of the rhesus monkey
- How many turkeys are there in Turkey
- Wolfram, what is the probability of a straight flush
- Wolfram, pound sign F-F-3-3-C-C
- Give me a random number

Doing Math

Figure 5.6   Simple arithmetic

Siri can help you do your simple, day-to-day math for you. Whether it be a quick estimate of your shopping budget, sorting out a tip on your meal or even splitting up the dinner bill, Siri will be there at your service.

The basic mathematical functions are intuitive to use. "Add 220 and 360.36" or "What's 220 plus 360.36" will both give you the results of those numbers. You can do the same with "minus" or "take away", "times" or "multiply", and "divide". This will work with decimals and fractions too.

Siri comes in especially handy when dividing up the dinner bill. For example, if you have a bill of $220.70 with a service charge or tip of 15% to divide among 8 people, you can use the command "What's $220.70 with a 15% tip for eight people?" This will give you a total of $31.73 per person, along with the total bill.

Siri will even let you know if you're in a country where tipping is not customary!

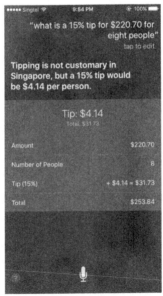

Figure 5.7   No need for a tip

Currency

If you find yourself overseas unsure about how much that hotel stay or gadget will cost in your home currency, Siri can help you out. If you refer to an ambiguous currency like "dollars", Siri will take into account your current location to infer which currency you're referring to, so remember to include the country name before the currency if necessary.

- How much is 100 euros in pounds
- How much is 100 US dollars in Brazilian riel

Converting between currencies is easy to do, but make sure you phrase your question properly and use the right currency to get the right result. Starting your question with "What is" may prompt Siri to perform a web search instead.

Show me some stocks

You walk past an Apple store, see the throngs of customers and think: The company must be doing pretty well. While Siri can't serve as your voice-assisted broker (yet?) or recommend a stock, it can help pull up stock quotes and basic information very quickly.

Figure 5.8   How is Apple doing right now?

To find out the stock price for a company, just ask Siri about it, such as "How is Apple doing right now" or "What is Amazon's stock price". Siri can also give you an overview of the major stock indices (tailored to your local area). If you want more information, just tap on the display and Siri will launch the Stocks app on the iPhone. The information is provided by Yahoo! Finance. You can visit the related site by tapping on the Yahoo! icon on the bottom right of the display.

Here are some commands that you can use with Siri:

- How are the markets today
- What is the Hang Seng Index at today
- Show me the FTSE 100
- Where did the DJIA close at today
- What is Amazon trading at
- What is Apple's P/E ratio
- What is Microsoft's dividend yield
- What is Google's high this year
- What did Tesla close at yesterday

Note that Siri's ability to retrieve historical data is limited to the most recent closing price. It cannot obtain stock information that goes beyond that.

Figure 5.9   An overview of the markets

Finding Your Way Around

Apple Maps was introduced in 2012 and replaced Google Maps as the default map application in its devices. While it faced much criticism in its early days due to numerous errors, it has improved by leaps and bounds since.

Maps is integrated with Siri, making it easy to get directions from your phone without even having to unlock your phone. This extends to more than just calculating the route between two fixed addresses. Maps can help you find amenities nearby, such as petrol stations / gas stations, ATMs or even restaurants of a specific cuisine.

This functionality is also integrated with your Contacts, so you can give instructions such as "Take me home" and "Direct me to Steve's office", which will access the addresses stored in your contact list.

To start your journey, tell Siri to guide you to your destination with the commands "Direct me to", "Take me to" or "Show me the directions to", followed by your destination address. Siri will open up the Maps application within the Siri interface and start the navigation immediately. You can specify a different origin address instead: "Take me from 1600 Pennsylvania Avenue to Mt Evans".

On the top of your screen, you will find the estimated distance

Figure 5.10   To Steve's place!

to your destination, the duration of your journey, and estimated arrival time. The estimated time of arrival (ETA) and duration of the journey is calculated based on the speed limit along the way, so keep that in mind when you plan your trip.

There are also options to show the map in 3D, a list of all the steps required, as well as an overview of the entire journey. In the overview mode, you can tweak the map to explore your journey. Tap on the small arrow on the bottom left to move back to your starting location and reposition the map in the right direction.

Maps provides turn-by-turn navigation, allowing you to receive directions while you keep your eyes on the road. Once you have begun your journey, you can ask journey-specific questions, such as "What's my ETA". You can even ask Siri the hallowed question, "Are we there yet?"

Figure 5.11   Are we there yet?

Look at specific locations using Siri. The instructions "Show me 1600 Pennsylvania Avenue" or "Show me the Eiffel Tower" will give you a map with your desired location pinned on it. You can also get your current location by asking Siri "Where am I?"

In my opinion, one of the most useful features is the ability to search for shops or facilities around you. Siri is able to interpret the context around a question, and use it to recommend places that fit your needs. Do note, however, that certain local details may not be recognised or available on the map. For example, I was unable to find ATMs from a bank that was not local .

Figure 5.12   Finding an ATM

The following commands will return recommendations that match your criteria as closely as possible, along with details such as ratings, price and distance.

- I need a haircut
- I need some medicine
- I need a doctor
- What's a coffee place near me
- Find me a place with happy hour
- Find me a place to eat where I can sit outside
- I want an inexpensive restaurant
- Find me a restaurant that serves Indian food
- I'm running low on petrol/gas
- Where is the nearest ATM
- I need a Citibank ATM

Maps is a work in progress, and users have given feedback about its sometimes erratic performance. In many areas (especially out of the US), the Maps functionality is not as developed as other alternatives, and may not provide as much detail. If the ease and convenience of using Siri with Maps does not seem like much of an improvement to you, other map applications or dedicated GPS devices may provide better detail about your route.

With iOS 9, Maps now includes transit directions in some cities:

- London
- New York

- San Francisco Bay Area
- Toronto
- Baltimore
- Berlin
- Chicago
- Mexico City
- Philadelphia
- Washington DC
- 300 cities in China, including Beijing, Shanghai, Shenzhen, and Guangzhou

SPORTS & ENTERTAINMENT
Sports, Music and Books

In iOS 6, Siri learnt sports-speak, bringing up scores and sports-related tidbits. Since then, Siri has expanded its sports coverage with a wider range of sports leagues and information.

Figure 6.1   Siri doesn't like hockey..

Besides sports, Siri also knows about movies, helping you to find the latest films and screens near you.

Siri can also help you control your music. The early iterations of Siri included integration with the Music app and help with song recognition. Along with the much-anticipated launch of Apple Music, Siri's capabilities on this front have expanded greatly. You can now search for songs and get recommendations based on your preferences.

Figure 6.2   Serenade me, Siri

Sports

Siri is a huge sports fan! Since iOS 6, Siri has featured support for sports-related queries, allowing you to tap on it to check on sports events, real-time scores, fixtures, or tidbits to settle that bet with your friends.

Figure 6.3   How're the Yankees?

Siri's sporting prowess is the result of a partnership with Yahoo! Sports, giving you access to a range of sports, including baseball, American football, basketball, ice hockey, and soccer (or football). Unfortunately, that's the limit to Siri's capability. It supports mostly sports popular in the US, leaving out other widely-played sports such as cricket, tennis or rugby.

That said, if you're into a sport that Siri plays, Siri can be a great help in retrieving information about it. You can start by looking up scores of past or live games. To do that, just ask Siri "What's the score of the San Antonio Spurs game?" or "How is the Cubs game going?"

Siri covers the following leagues.

- American football: NCAA College Football, National Football League
- Baseball: Major League Baseball
- Basketball: NCAA College Basketball, National Basketball Association, Women's National Basketball Association
- Football: Bundesliga, Dutch Eredivisie, Ligue 1, Serie A, J League, La Liga, Liga MX, Major League Soccer, English Premier League, Swiss Super League

Besides regular league sports, Siri also covers major football tournaments, such as the Champions League, Europa League, and World Cup Qualifiers.

Siri knows where you are and tailors its answers accordingly. For example, asking Siri about football outside of the U.S. will prompt a list of association football teams, instead of NFL teams. This also affects Siri's ability to look up the shorter version of a team's name. Searching for scores of the "Cubs game" will give you the score for the current or previous game played by the Chicago Cubs. However, if you search for the "Spurs", you might get a result for a Tottenham Hotspur game instead.

Figure 6.4   When're the Spurs playing?

When looking up a specific game, Siri will show you some game information, including the stadium and city where it was played, the logos of each team, the score, date and names of players who scored. This differs based on each sport. Looking up a Yankees game will give you the score every inning, while

while looking up an NBA game will give you the score every quarter.

If you look up a match from a playoff or tournament, Siri will include information about the tournament or the running score of the playoffs. Here are some ways to ask Siri about scores.

- How was Liverpool's last game
- How did the San Antonio Spurs fare
- What's the score of the Cubs game
- Did the Yankees win last night
- How is DC United doing today
- When was Barcelona's last game
- What was the score between the Red Sox and the Twins
- Show me all the NFL scores from last week
- Show me English Premier League scores from last season
- I want NBA scores from last month

Of course, Siri can give you more than just the scores. It can access details about each league and their corresponding teams. For example, if it's the off-season, you can ask Siri "When does the NBA season start?"

If you're planning to catch a game on the television later, you can check "What baseball games are scheduled for today?" or "Is there an NFL game today?" You can also check on when the game starts by asking "What time is the LA Lakers' game?"

Figure 6.5   When does the season start?

Look up your favourite team by asking "When is LA Galaxy playing?" or "Show me DC United's fixtures." You can also check on the league by asking "When is the NHL season's first game?" or "When does the Bundesliga start?"

Keep track of your team's roster of players. Siri can look up the names of all the players in your team, along with information such as shirt numbers, positions and photograph if available. You can also tap on each player's name to get more information about his physical statistics or game statistics. Do this with "Show me the Miami Heat" or "Show me Manchester United's roster".

Figure 6.6   Look up team rosters

If you want information about just one player alone, ask Siri for it. "Show me Kobe Bryant" or "Show me Kevin Durant's stats".

Siri can even check on injuries in your favourite team! Just ask "Is anyone in the New York Yankees injured?" or "Is LeBron James injured?"

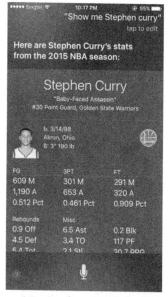

Figure 6.7   Look up individual players

If you're a fan of statistics or just looking to settle a bet, you can ask Siri about team and player information.

- Which team scored he most points in the NBA
- Show me the NBA standings
- Who has the most goals in Bayern Munich
- Who has the highest slugging percentage in the Yankees
- What is the Texas Rangers' away record
- Who has the most points on the Oilers

- Who has the most homeruns on the Giants
- Who is taller, Stephen Curry or Anthony Davis

Figure 6.8   Find out who's injured

Movies

Your virtual assistant can do more than just manage your time and schedule. It can help you plan your downtime too. Siri has partnered with Rotten Tomatoes to bring to you movie facts, showtimes and reviews so you know what to watch and where.

With Siri, find movies playing at theatres near you by asking "What movies are showing near me?" or just "What's showing near me?" Siri will provide you with a list of movies, showtimes, trailers and even reviews! You can also search for movies somewhere else, by including a new location in your question.

Search for a specific movie by saying "Show me showtimes for The Avengers". If you don't have anything in mind, you can look up current movies by searching through themes or studios. For example, "What comedies are currently showing?" or "Show me movies by Paramount". If you have your kids with you, you can also search by film restrictions, such as "What PG movies are playing tomorrow?" or film type with "Are there 3D movies showing near me?"

You won't always know what you want to watch. Trailers are a good way to start looking! Get your trailers with Siri by saying "Show me a trailer for The Grand Budapest Hotel". This might not always work, however, depending on the trailer availability and your location.

Figure 6.9   Specify, specify!

Trying to decide between two movies? With Rotten Tomatoes, you can get "freshness" scores straight from Siri. For example, ask Siri "Show me reviews for The Theory of Everything" or "How are the reviews for Selma" to get a quick score, along with some qualitative reviews.

Movies are great fodder for parties and games. When you find yourself trying desperately to recall a movie fact, you can turn to Siri for help. Siri can give you film details, such as directors, actors and film awards. Here are some things you can ask Siri.

Figure 6.10   Easy way to view trailers

- Who directed Mad Max: Fury Road?
- Who starred in American Sniper?
- Which movie won Best Picture in 2000?
- Who won Best Actor in 1988?

Siri is a good tool for quickly looking up reviews and movie showtimes. However, film schedules and other movie-related features are not available in all countries yet, although this list is expected to expand with future iOS updates. The movie tidbit feature isn't perfect either, but if Siri cannot help, it will offer to do a web search or show you the Rotten Tomatoes page for your movie instead.

Nonetheless, movie integration with Siri looks promising, so hang on tight. In the future, Siri might even be able to help you book your tickets online!

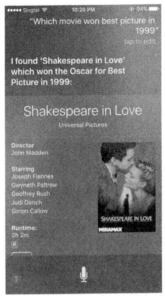

Figure 6.11   Search for movie tidbits

Music

The Control Centre was launched with iOS 7, giving you quick access to your main settings and toggles, including a control panel for your music. With Siri, you can now perform the same functions (and more) with your voice. Siri allows you to play any song, artist, album or playlist on command, so you don't have to scroll through your Music app to find your favourite songs.

Apple Music was released with iOS 8.4 and is very deeply integrated with iOS. Siri's capabilities has expanded alongside it, giving you some new commands to manage your playlist. This includes accessing radio stations and music charts, queuing your playsts, add music to your library, among other things.

But first up, some basic functions. To play a particular song, just use the keyword "Play" and tell Siri which song to play. You can also do this with specific artists, albums, playlists or even genres.

- Play "Fix You"
- Play songs by Coldplay
- Play Pablo Honey by Radiohead
- Play my Workout playlist
- Play some hip-hop

Siri expands on your basic control functions, letting you query the current song or artist, and accessing iTunes' Genius feature to play similar songs, or favourite your songs.

Figure 6.12   Play your songs with one word

- Play
- Pause
- Skip
- Next song
- Previous song
- What is this song
- Who sings this
- Play music similar to this
- Shuffle my music (This will play all songs)

Figure 6.13   Play more songs like this

- Buy this song
- Add this track to my wishlist
- Get the new Coldplay album

Apple Music now gives you several new commands to use with Siri. Tune into the new Apple radio stations by saying "Play Beats 1" or "Play Chill". You can customise your very own playlist and listening experience by adjusting the mix with "I like this song", "Play more songs like this" or "Don't play this again".

If you like listening to podcasts instead, Siri can also help you with that. Like your music playlist, simply tell Siri to "Play my podcasts" or "Play the Serial podcast" to launch your favourite episodes. If your podcasts are not already on your device, you can get it by saying "Download the latest 99% Invisible podcast".

You can search through music charts to find the best music from a different time, the most popular music from a specific band, or even the soundtrack from a particular movie. Apple Music also allows you to queue music, letting you decide on which song to

Figure 6.14   Hook me up!

play next.

Before Apple Music, Siri could help you kick off your very own playlists. Now, Siri can also call up Apple-curated playlists or play you the latest songs from a specific artist. If you like the album, you can add it to your library!

Siri also knows Billboard charts, so pull up the greatest songs in history and kick back. Siri can play the top songs by genre, years, months, specific dates or artists.

If you ask Siri to play a song, it will belt out the original or most well-known version. To get a specific version, include the artist in your instruction. You can even ask Siri to play a song from a movie, and it'll try to get that specific cover! Not to worry, this will work just as well for TV shows too.

Here are some commands to get you familiar:
- Play Beats 1
- Play more songs like this
- Don't play this again
- Play the top songs from 1985
- Play the top album by Ellie Goulding
- Play songs from Lord of the Rings
- After this song, play "Paper Boats"
- Play the Selma playlist
- Play playlist Intro to Carcass

Figure 6.15   Play your favourite playlists

Ever been in a checkout line when a great song comes on? Had trouble trying to recognise those songs? Besides looking up songs from you, Siri can help you identify songs using Shazam. When you hear a song you want to identify, just ask Siri "What song is this?" or "What's that?" It will listen and give you the song title and artist.

Books

Apple has been expanding iBooks, its ebook library and reader. The iBooks Store now features over 2.5 million books, letting you access your favourite authors and works from the convenience of your device. For example, to look up books by Charles Dickens in the store, simply say "Find books by Charles Dickens". You can also access books by saying "Get the latest Stephen King book".

Figure 6.16   Enable Speak Screen

Make Siri read a book (awkwardly) to you! This can be done by making use of your device's accessibility features. To enable this, go to Settings -> General -> Accessibility -> Speech and turn on "Speak Screen". With this enabled, your phone will read out a selection when you swipe down with two fingers from the top of your screen. Open up an e-book (PDF versions don't work very well with this), swipe with two fingers to the bottom of your screen, and enjoy!

DICTATION
Reading to you

Ever pictured yourself sitting back in a recliner with your eyes closed, speaking aloud while your assistant fervently hammers out your speech or story on a clickety typewriter? With Siri's help, you can do that with ease.

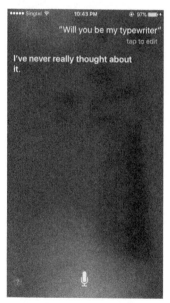

Figure 7.1   Be my typewriter

It's easy to use Dictation on your iOS device. Dictation can be used anywhere you can enter text. On your keyboard, there will be a small microphone symbol next to the spacebar. Tap on the microphone and start dictating!

The keyboard will be replaced by a feedback pattern that shows you whether anything is received. The louder you speak, the more the feedback waves will jump, so speak louder if it isn't moving much. Your text should appear as you speak, with only a very slight delay.

Making the most of Dictation

Dictation understands basic text commands and punctuation. Some of these commands have already been covered in **Keeping in Touch**. More commands can be found at the back of the book.

Figure 7.2   Something wrong there

Siri learns as you speak. The more you use it, the better it will understand you, and adapt to your voice and accent. Like the rest of Siri, its privacy settings means that this information is lost when you reset Siri on your device.

In iOS, words that are flagged by the auto-correct feature will be underlined with a squiggly blue line. Tapping on the word that is underlined will give you a list of replacements to choose from.

One requirement

Like regular use of Siri, the Dictation feature will only work if you are connected to the internet. As you dictate, your voice message is transmitted to Apple's servers where it is interpreted before being returned to your device. If you are keen on dictating your 360-page book all at one go, make sure you are connected to a strong WiFi connection for Dictation to serve you better.

LAST WORDS
The Future of Siri

Siri has changed much since its first launch. Along with the suite of Apple devices and services, Siri is set to take on ever-growing roles, turning into a full-fledged personal assistant able to tell you what you need to know, even before you ask.

Figure 8.1   Boom and cats, try it!

Multi-Functional

With new health, home and fitness frameworks, among others, Siri could potentially become a multi-functional control for all things built on this platform. For example, perhaps your home appliances would in future be connected to your device, so you can turn on the lights or switch off specific appliances using your voice. Telling Siri "I'm going to bed" could let you shut down all operating appliances, leaving only the essential ones on, such as bedroom lighting and the heater.

Figure 8.2   Goodnight, Siri

iOS 9 has brought Proactive to Siri, a feature that is capable of processing contextual information to predict what you need or want, and serve up those without prompting. For instance, it can download the latest issue of your virtual morning newspaper based on your daily routine, or tell you when it's time to leave for the airport based on a boarding ticket stored on your phone and traffic information.

Proactive can access your most-used apps, to learn about your routine, serving up your apps when you want them, such as showing you a link to your Twitter app if you check it everyday as you leave home. Siri is an integral part of this new framework, leveraging on its integration with your device's built-in services.

Offline and Plugged In

Siri is not yet "on-board" your device, which means it requires Internet access in order to process your voice command. Even mundane and local tasks, such as changing your settings or alarms, require you to be online. This could affect the rollout of Siri's capabilities elsewhere, as it makes Siri's features dependent on network performance and availability.

In contrast, Google Now released an update in 2014 to support offline access to Google Now cards, meaning that local apps that did not require an Internet access would be available even if you lost network service. Siri might incorporate a similar feature in future updates, allowing you to access certain local functions without access to the Internet, although that would mean having to move its voice-parsing tool on-device.

Siri used to feature a Raise to Speak setting, where you could activate Siri just by bringing your phone to your ear. This mode is unavailable in the current version, although users have voiced support for it, claiming that it makes it easier to activate when driving or doing something else. With iOS 8, "Hey Siri" made its entrance, allowing you to issue a command to Siri hands-free. This has since been improved as the hardware in Apple's devices evolved, now letting you command Siri even when you're not plugged in.

Development and Usability

While Siri has been quite a success, there is still no Siri API available for developers. That said, it seems unlikely that Apple would release an API anytime soon, at least before it completes its rollout of core Apple functions. Siri's success has been contingent on its voice recognition, ability to contextualise commands and responding accurately. Besides, Siri processes certain commands through third-party services, such as Rotten Tomatoes, Open Table and Bing. An API might pose technical and business-side issues that may derail Siri's success or development track.

Figure 8.3　Hot, hot, hot

Siri's ease of usability on Apple's mobile devices have raised questions about when Siri will make a transition onto Mac OS X computers. There have been rumours of integration testing with OS X, although nothing concrete has been mentioned yet. OS X Yosemite brought certain changes that seemed to simulate Siri's responses, albeit with typed input and without voice control. This could be Apple slowly fine-tuning its ability to generate suitable results on OS X, which boasts a far larger and more unstructured environment compared to its mobile devices with their limited functionality.

OS X Yosemite featured Continuity, which allowed integration between a user's devices. With Continuity, you could keep your browser consistent across devices, perform calls and send text messages with non-mobile devices, and even continue on e-mails using another device. This could be a way to introduce Siri in a limited fashion for the OS X, by allowing voice commands that are limited to features already found on the iOS.

One potential feature may tap Siri's voice recognition talents to create another layer of security using a voice version of Touch ID. While this would not be a revolutionary feature in itself, a Voice ID could improve Siri's performance by allowing a user to unlock his/her device while giving a command to activate Siri. This enables the user to bypass having to unlock the device when accessing certain features with Siri.

Using vocal signatures would solve the problem of the generic "Hey Siri" activation method. In its current form, shouting "Hey Siri" in a crowded room may activate several devices at once. Having voice recognition would ensure activation only when the vocal input matches the stored voice signature.

The Future

Siri is the subject of many rumours about iOS 10. One feature

Figure 8.4   Siri can you be Google?

that has been taken seriously is the integration of Siri with voicemail, allowing Siri to answer calls for you or transcribe a text message. One other rumour concerns customising user profiles for different users of a single device.

When Proactive was launched in iOS 9, it was widely seen as disappointing when set against the high expectations for it. As we build up toward iOS 10, I expect it to bring a great deal more functionality to Proactive, including more app integration and proactive suggestions. This could range from simple things like better management of your Contacts, to actively suggesting timeslots for meetings based on your calendar and history of contact with a person.

Siri's role in HomeKit could become integral to building a wholesome iOS experience, allowing your device to interact with other home devices and appliances. This would mark a big step up for Siri, and put it on a path away from being a simple phone assistant and toward a full-time personal assistant.

The future of Siri stretches as far as what you can dream of. Siri has taken on an important role in Apple's devices, helping you to complete your tasks with ease, whether it be setting a reminder, making your routine accessible, or guiding you home. With each iteration of Siri comes the promise of much more, and I am eager and excited to be part of this evolution.

Till then!

Figure 8.5   Bye Siri!

REFERENCE
Quick Guide to Siri's Commands

Siri is not all work and no play. It has a lighter side that appears when you play around with your questions. This reference chapter will give you a quick summary of the various commands covered in the previous chapters, along with some fun commands that you can try out. Siri can tell jokes too, just like a real assistant!

Contacts

Joe Dugan is my father
Lindy is my sweetheart
Show Mitch Hamilton
Find people named Mark
Who is Jen Gray?
When is my husband's birthday?
What is Priscilla's mobile phone number?
Find Jamie's email address
Find my father's home address
Is my wife home?

Where is Emily?

Is there anyone near me?

Let me know when my husband has left work

Calendar

Set up a 9AM meeting

Meet with Daphne at 8PM tonight at the Road Bar

Schedule a meeting about promotion at 1030AM tomorrow

Move my 9AM meeting to 11AM

Cancel the planning meeting tomorrow

Add Graham to my 3PM meeting

What's on my calendar next Tuesday?

When is my meeting with Tony?

Where is my next meeting?

Show me today's schedule

What is my next appointment?

Applications

Open Email

Open Photos

Open Messages

Show me my Settings

Alarm & Timer

Set an alarm for 7AM
Show me my alarms
Delete all my alarms
Delete my 8AM alarm
Wake me up in 6 hours

Set the timer for an hour
Show the timer
Pause the timer
Reset it
Resume the timer
Stop the timer

Dates

What is today's date?
What is the date next Monday?
What time is it in Chicago?
What time is it now?
Tell me the time now.

Calls and Facetime

Facetime Lenny
Call Major John

Notes

Note that tomorrow is the deadline
Note this
Find my notes on the carpool
Show me my notes from last Tuesday
Add lettuce to my shopping list
Add pay the bills to my to-do list
Remind me about this when I get to the car
Remind me to call Liam at 6PM
Remind me to bring home the bacon

Search

Search for best keyboards in 2016
Search for carbonara recipes
Wikipedia January Jones
Search for the iPhone 7 launch date

Twitter

Tweet with my location "Looks like a great day today!"
Post to Twitter "Another day at the beach" hashtag beachbum
Tweet "Happy birthday Andy"

Weather

What's the weather today?
What's the weather going to be like tomorrow?
What is the weather forecast for next week in Wellington?
What's the high for Sydney this Friday?
How windy is it now?
Will it rain tonight?
What time is sunrise in Milan?
What is the windchill here?
What is the UV index now?
Will it snow in Boston this week?

Emails & Messages

Do I have any new messages?
Reply "I don't care"
Call her
Text Katie "Are you almost here?"
Send a message to Jimmy on his mobile saying it's okay
Read my new messages

Show me my emails
Do I have new mail?
Show me the email from Eric yesterday
Show me the email about the school bus

Read me my emails
Write a new email to Jason
Email Jason about the trip tomorrow
Email my boyfriend and say I received the package today

Navigation

Show me the nearest coffeeshop
Is there a petrol kiosk nearby?
Find me a gas station
Good steakhouses around here
I want some Chinese food
Give me directions to Los Angeles
Take me home
Are we there yet?
What's my ETA?
Is there a gas station on the route home?

Reservations & Reviews

Make a reservation at a Spanish restaurant tonight at 8PM
Show me the reviews for Blue Note
Table for six at the Barbelle tonight at 7PM

Sports

How is the Yankees game going?
What is the score of the Lakers game?
Show me the English Premier League table
How was Liverpool's last game?
When is DC United's next game?
Show me all the NFL scores from this week
I want NBA scores from last month
When does the NFL season start?
Show me the San Antonio Spurs
Show me Chelsea's roster
Is LeBron James injured?
Who is taller, Stephen Curry or Antony Davis?
What is the Texas Rangers' away record?
Who has the most homeruns on the Giants?
Who has the highest slugging percentage in the Yankees?

Movies

Search for Disney movies
What romantic comedies are in theatres today?
What's playing at the cinema today?
What's playing at Capitol Theatre tomorrow?
Show me reviews for Zootopia.
Who directed The Great Gatsby?

I want to watch the latest Disney movie
Who won Best Actor in 2015?

Music

Play "Fix it" by Coldplay
Play my Jazz playlist
I want to listen to some blues
Shuffle my studying playlist
Pause
Skip
Play

Stocks

How are the markets today?
Show me the Dow Jones
What is the Hang Seng Index at today?
What is Apple's P/E ratio?
What is Google's high this year?
What did Amazon close at yesterday?
What is IBM's dividend yield?

Fun

I love you
Do you love me?
Will you marry me?
I feel lonely
Do you believe in Christmas?
When is Santa coming to town?
When is Thanksgiving?
I need drugs
Where can I hide a body?
I have to poop
I don't like your tone
Can you find the email I sent tomorrow?
Good morning Siri (try this at night)
Talk dirty to me
I'm drunk

Who are you?
What is your name?
Do you have family?
What do you like to do?
What is your favourite number/colour?
How are you, Siri?
Who's your daddy?
How old are you?

When is your birthday?
Happy birthday Siri
Are you human?
Are you real?
How do you feel now?
Who is your favourite person?
What languages do you speak, Siri?
What are you wearing?
Are you a girl or a boy?
You're wonderful
You're my best friend
What do you think about Android?
Do I look fat?
Ha ha
Why does my husband/wife hate me?
Tell me a joke
Tell me a story
Sing to me
Do you want to know a secret?
Knock knock

What is the meaning of life?
What is love?
What is evil?
What are you?

Does God exist?
Do you believe in hell?

Take me to your leader
Who is your leader?
Who let the dogs out?
Flip a coin
Why did the chicken cross the road?
I can't let you do that, Dave
Open the pod bay doors
Do you know HAL 9000?

Formatting

New line	Inserts a line break and starts on a new line (equivalent to pressing Enter on a keyboard)
New paragraph	Starts on a new paragraph
Cap	Capitalise the next word
Caps on	Capitalises the first letter of each word
Caps off	Turn off "Caps on"
All caps	Next word will be in all upper case
All caps on	Turn on Caps Lock
All caps off	Turn off Caps Lock
No caps	Make next word lower case
No caps on	All words will be in lower case
No caps off	Turn off "No caps off"
Space bar	Prevents hyphen from appearing in a hyphenated word
No space	No space between words
No space on	Stop adding spaces to your instructions. This helps with spelling your word if it's not easily recognised

No space off	Revert to normal spaces between words
Quote... end quote	Places quotation marks around a section of text
Open single quote... close single quote	Places single quotation marks around a section of text

Punctuation

Period / dot	.
Comma	,
Colon	:
Semi-colon	;
Exclamation mark / point	!
Inverted exclamation mark / point	¡
Question mark	?
Inverted question mark	¿
Apostrophe	'
Ellipsis / dot dot dot	...
Hyphen / dash	-
Em dash	–
Underscore	_
Open parenthesis	(
Close parenthesis	)

Open bracket	[
Close bracket	]
Open brace	{
Close brace	}
Open angle bracket	<
Close angle bracket	>
Quote / quotation mark	"
Single quote	'

Typography

Ampersand	&
At sign	@
Asterisk	*
Slash / forward slash	/
Backward slash	\
Caret	¡
Centre dot	•
Degree sign	°
Pound sign / hashtag	#
Vertical bar	|
Underscore	_
Percent sign	%

Mathematical Functions

Plus sign	+
Minus sign	-
Equals sign	=
Multiplication sign	x
Greater than sign	>
Lesser than sign	<
Percent sign	%

Symbols

Copyright sign	©
Registered sign	®
Trademark sign	™
Section sign	§

Currency

Euro sign	€
Yen sign	¥
Dollar sign	$
Pound sterling sign	£
Cent sign	¢

Smileys

Smiley / smile face	:-)
Frowny / frown face	:-(
Winky / wink face	;-)
Cross-eyed laughing face	XD

Shortforms

E G	e.g.
I E	i.e.

Siri can also produce smileys with "smiley face", "frowny face" or "wink face". Reading out the letters "e g" or "i e" will produce "e.g." and "i.e." respectively.

INDEX

Printed in Great Britain
by Amazon